100 Tips & Strategies to bolster your personal brand.

My Story

I always had a passion for making my projects popular.

In 2012 I launched my first project with Infinity Downline as an Affiliate Marketer, where I used Instagram as promotion platform where I was able to sell memberships and make thousands of dollars utilizing Instagram effectively while building a tribe.

A couple years later I joined a Network Marketing company called WakeUpNow where I built a team of 100+ distributors, became one of the youngest top earner in the company. They flew me out to Salt Lake City, Utah where I met with millionaires and network with some of the worlds top entrepreneurs, speakers & marketing influencers.

2017 I graduated from Georgia Northwestern Technical College with a major in Marketing Management with specialization in Entrepreneurship.

Instead of working for a company after college I decided to start my own now I'm here promoting it JMA, Jalen Marketing Agency, LLC. Our goal is to help local biusness & brands, increase revenue by levraging their social media platforms & brand story.

Disclaimer

Contents

Characteristic

1. Attitude. Your altitude in life will always be direct reflection of your attitude.

2. Appearance. They say don't judge a book by it's cover but we do anyways so always dress for the part you want.

3. Be ambitious. Stay focused on the financial rewards & achievements that awaits you on the other side.

4. Believe in yourself. If you don't believe in yourself who else will? Success starts with you.

5. Be self-motivated. If you want to be successful entrepreneur, you should always motivate yourself to work harder.

6. Be purpose driven or goal oriented. Aspire to something greater than self, develop magnificent obsession.

7. Be disciplined. Keep yourself on track to follow your plans and goals.

8. Be respectful and open to change. You cannot plan every single twist and turn for a new business from the beginning. Often time's setbacks will occur that will require you to take a different path than the one you planned on. Be open to change, as long as your initial goal remains intact.

9. Ownership. Give you rights over property, land, real estate etc. When owning you can rent out and make money or you can pass down to family member for years and build generational wealth.

10. Don't QUIT Never! You are going to have skeptics and none believers. People are naturally skeptical. Skeptical of new products, services, new ideas and competition.

Customer/Clients

1. Under promise and over deliver. Never promise more than you can deliver. It's always better to exceed customers expectation than to disappoint them.

2. Customer service is everything. If you can service your customers when they have a problem or need help, you will have a very high customer retention rate.

3. Put yourself in their shoes. Love your neighbor as yourself.

4. Be the expert. Give your clients a quick courtesy call inform them of upcoming changes and provide some insightful recommendations as best plan of attack becoming a trusted source on all. You build a relationship that leads to a dependency your customers will trust you as apart of their success.

5. Build trust through relationships. As the age old saying goes, you do business with people you like and trust. Trust is essential in business and building relationships with clients will garner your trust.

6. Build relationships online. Your clients are online, so lets start building relationships with them. While they are glued to their computer screens or cell phone.

7. Go above and beyond. Going the extra mile for your customers will set you apart from the masses and easy way to build strong relationships. As a service business, you have countless opportunities to wow your clients.

8. Listen to your customers. Implementing customer feedback survey forms, or just asking question can help you keep the asking question can help you keep the customers happy.

9. Set customers expectations. The first step to building customer relations is to set clients expectations early. The earlier the better. Don't wait.

10. Adding value. The value you bring to them goes far beyond just your products. Help them with services that you do not provide.

Economics

1. Utilize all of your resources. Never be shy or scared to use any and every resource that is possibly available to you.

2. Time is money. A old saying which means your time is valuable, so don't waste it. If you want to 10x your time and leverage and get more done in less time pay others to do time consuming task.

3. Cash is king. The belief that money cash is more valuable than any other form of investment tool. You need to carefully watch your cash flow and do whatever it takes to maximize every dollar that is spent. Credit is Queen.

4. Lord of your land. Being a landlord instead of a tenant is the difference between driving a Lamborghini or Lincoln.

5. Network equal net worth. It's not what you know, but whom you know. This old adage is truer now than ever before. If you're motivated to become wealthy or be successful in any endeavor, your ability to create and leverage resources is unquestionably one of the critical keys to success.

6. If I spend this dollar will it make me a dollar. This is a great question to ask yourself every time you spend money. Always see if the money that is being spent can be justified otherwise think again.

7. Limit what you borrow. You can't borrow or buy your way to wealth. So be careful with loans and credit cards. If you get in over your head, negotiate with your lenders to pay what you can. Once you're debt free. Save money & start investing.

8. Perception paradigm. How you look at the world and how the world looks at you.

9. Don't spend what you don't have. Buy smart look for deals. The smart ones live on a comfortable middle class spending plan.

10. Economic disaster. Begins with a philosophy of doing less and wanting more.

Development

1. Read a book everyday. Books are concentrated sources of wisdom. The more books you read, the more wisdom you expose yourself too. One book I've read and found useful. Think & Grow Rich

2. Overcome your fears. All of us have fears. Fear of uncertainty, fear of public speaking, fear of risk. All our fears keep us in the same position and prevent us from growing. Recognize that your fears reflect areas where you can grow.

3. Wake up early. Waking up earlier say '5-6' has been acknowledged by many self help gurus to improve your productivity and your quality of life.

4. Get out of your comfort zone. Real growth comes with hard work and sweat. Being too comfortable doesn't help us grow. It makes us stagnant.

5. Avoid negative people. As my mentor says Jim Rohn you are the average of the 5 people you spend the most time with.

6. Get mentor or coach. There is no faster way to improve than to have someone work with you on your goals.

7. Let go of the past. A bend in the road is not the end of the road unless you fail to make the turn.

8. Start a journal. Journals are great way to gain better selfawareness. It's a self-reflective process. As you write, clarify your thought process and read what you wrote from a third person perspective. You gain more insights about yourself. I use my personal development blog as a personal journal too and I've learned a lot about myself through the last six months blogging.

9. Quit bad habits cultivate new habits. Good new habits to cultivate. 1, reading books 2, waking up early 3, exercising 4, meditate etc.

10. Start a new business venture. Start a 30 day challenge. Set a goal and give yourself 30 days to achieve it.

Knowledge

1. A degree is just a piece of paper. To be a entrepreneur, you don't need some sort of degree or qualification. You just need to love what you do.

2. Start small but think big. Start small and work your way up, but always keep your big goals and aspirations in mind.

3. Keep learning. Regardless of how much knowledge you posses or successful you are, it is important to keep educating yourself on your markets.

4. Read, Listen, Learn. Make sure you have a culture where you never think you know enough. Be open to learning and hungry for knowledge, whether the people are younger, older in different places or culture groups.

5. Surround yourself with smart people. If you are hanging around smart people and involving yourself in intellectual conversations on a regular basis, your mind will grow.

6. Accept criticism. Criticism isn't always the best thing to hear, but you have to accept it. Criticism is important if you want to improve yourself & business.

7. Experience over education. You will learn more about business within a month of starting your company then you will in all your years at a business school.

8. Measure to improve business performance. How do your knowledge add value to your organization or company.

9. Knowledge management. John Maxwell said change is inevitable, growth is optional.

10. Never stop learning. Formal education will make you a living but self education will make you a fortune.

Marketing

1. Be authentic. When branding and promoting yourself be transparent. The real you will always get the best results.

2. Be unique. If you can stand out in this world, people may hate you but many others will love you.

3. Create visuals. The world loves visualization rather than read. Creating demos, videos and slideshows. So potential customers can visualize what you offer.

4. Selling. No matter what market you are entering, you are going need to sell. Watch great sellers in action and gain your selling style.

5. Your phone is a powerful business tool. If you know how to harness it correctly smartphones offer numerous advantages to those who know how to use them well.

6. Think globally. Even though your located in one country does not mean you have to rely solely on the sales from that one country.

7. Start local. Local customers are quick and important start to building your business.

8. Sex sells. If you can make your product appealing as possible it's well known fact it will sell itself.

9. Capitalize on trends. Trends are what people are buzzing about at that point in time. You can use the topics that are interested in as launching point or inspiration.

10. Test everything. Before revealing a product or service to your customers can visualize what you have to offer.

Mentors

1. Perspective and experience. A mentor can give you the benefit of his or her perspective and experience.

2. Think outside the box. A mentor can help you look at situations in new ways.

3. Define and reach long term goals. Mentors can help you define your career path and ensure that you don't focus and continue down the road even when you become distracted by day to day pressures.

4. Accountability. When you know you are meeting with your mentor, you ensure that all the tasks you discussed in your last meeting are completed.

5. Trusted colleagues to discuss issues. A mentor can be a great sounding board for all issues.

6. Champion. A mentor who knows you well can be a strong champion of your positive attributes. As mentee, it is important to build trust and prove yourself worthy.

7. Expand your contact and networks. A mentor can help expand your network of contacts and business acquaintances.

8. Open doors. Mentors can open doors within your company, in other companies or onto a board.

9. Inspire. Mentors whose work you admire can be a strong inspiration.

10. Work better. With the help of a good mentor, you can work more efficiently with a clearer view of the future you are trying to achieve.

Media

1. Sell your story. Be sure to sell your story so well that not only the media but others will be interested in reading more.

2. Influencers. Find active journalist via twitter or other social networks and contact them directly to get coverage. Earn reputation with good press release and endorsement from people who you trust.

3. Share at the best times. There may not be exact time to post, but posting frequently and staying relevant can help you.

4. The media is your friend. Even though the media spends a lot of there time portraying others negatively. They can be your friend when used wisely.

5. Be media savvy. It's good to know about appropriate media outlets that can benefit your startup and are willing to cover your company.

6. Be prepared. It's your interview, not the reporters.

7. Keep it simple. Reporters are looking for clear simple live stories.

8. Make it easy to find you. Be sure to promote your brand and website and contact information.

9. Get right to the pointe. People want to hear what you got to say so get your point across.

10. Provide access to more info. That your fans/ followers may want.

Media

Product/Service

1. Make a product that can sell itself. If your product can just sit on shelf and be appealing to consumers.

2. Solve problems. Find a problem in the market place with your product/service and solve it.

3. Prove your product. Prove yourself in the world. If you can show proof to other people on why your products work or is better than other things available, than success should be easy.

4. Speed is secondary to quality. When it comes to customer service that keeps people coming back, the research shows quality matters more than speed.

5. Get ideal customers to be VIP's. Research by Nunes on loyalty programs has shown that people love being VIP or gold members.

6. Choose the right platform. Best way to improve your online customer service efforts is to utilize the channel your customers most prefer.

7. Trends. If you can recognize what people need in the marketplace and create a product or service that is sure to innovate and become a trend.

8. Under promise over deliver. Every package that arrives on time or product that works as intended reinforces your customer trust in you.

9. Make it personal. Remember, you represent your product. You have to feel like you represent your product from the moment you awake until you go to sleep. Be the brand.

10. Make sure your product or service passes the criteria test.
　　1. It should be something valuable for the customers.
　　2. It has to be well defined.
　　3. It has to be different than the competition.

Productivity/ Time Management

1. Time is precious. Value your time and understand the importance of time management.

2. Take action. Action may not always bring happiness, but there is no happiness without action.

3. Focus on the hardest task first. In the morning get up early and start on it you will be more focused and energized to finish it.

4. Make a choice. Decide what it is you're going to do, who you are going to be and what you are going to do.

5. Plan your day. If you fail to plan, you plan to fail.

6. Own your time. Do not disturb practice owning your time by not answering phone calls, emails, social medias etc.

7. Budget your time. Figure out how much time you usually spend on activities and then create a weekly schedule to follow

8. Time. Don't waste it.

9. Know your deadline. Mark the deadlines out clearly in your calendar and organize so you know when to finish.

10. Sleep. Be sure to get a good night rest so your brain can perform at peak potential.

BONUS

The Entrepreneur

1. Timing is everything. Finding a hot market and launching when the buzz is just starting is a great way to be successful

2. Branding. Everyone including your customers are online. If you can't be found online make money will be difficult.

3. Blog. You need to blog for your business as much as possible. Blogs help business owners establish themselves as experts in their niche while giving information away for free.

4. Dress to impress. If you look good you feel good and your clients & customers also feel good about you.

5. Know your strength and weakness. Always leverage your strength and be aware of your weakness so you can defend yourself when most venerable.

6. Opportunities are once in a lifetime. If a big opportunity come across you jump on it.

7. Persistence pays. Nothing in the world can take the place of persistence. Talent will not, nothing is more common than unsuccessful men with talent.

8. Be a strong decision maker. Decision making is one of the most important parts of a business.

9. Charisma. You must be able to positively influence others emotionally, mentally and physically.

10. Know when to punt. Many people and business stubbornly and mistakenly refuse to adopt to new economics, business realties and technologies.

11. Practice makes perfect. Keep practicing on ways to improve your startup.

12. Complex thinking. Successful entrepreneurs have unusual capacity for connecting the dots, being able to see the big picture, how the elements should fall into place and the next logical step.

13. Do what makes money first. Prioritize your to do list and be sure to put income producing task first

14. Always have a plan B. If project takes a wrong turn be ready for another plan.

15. Just Do It. Nike slogan says, just do it. It's a true statement for entrepreneurs.

16. Know what your purpose is. Answer these three questions to become clearer on purpose. a. Why am I here ? b. Who am I ? c. Where am I going?

17. If you want it go get it. Success in anything requires a strong dedication and passion for coming out on top.

18. Reduce risk. Eliminate the riskier aspects of your business for later to ensure a steady cash flow in the early goings of your startup.

19. People make the person. When becoming entrepreneur you need to understand people are at the heart of your success.

20. Success takes time. Be willing to work long hours for little profit for the first two or three years.

Author

I always had a passion for making my projects popular.

In 2012 I launched my first project with Infinity Downline as an Affiliate Marketer, where I used Instagram as promotion platform where I was able to sell memberships and make thousands of dollars utilizing Instagram effectively while building a tribe.

A couple years later I joined a Network Marketing company called WakeUpNow where I built a team of 100+ distributors, became one of the youngest top earner in the company. They flew me out to Salt Lake City, Utah where I met with millionaires and network with some of the worlds top entrepreneurs, speakers & marketing influencers.

2017 I graduated from Georgia Northwestern Technical College with a major in Marketing Management with specialization in Entrepreneurship.

Instead of working for a company after college I decided to start my own now I'm here promoting it JMA, Jalen Marketing Agency, LLC. Our goal is to help local biusness & brands, increase revenue by levraging their social media platforms & brand story.

Thank you for taking time time to read my ebook I really hope you got a lot of value out of it.

I have 1,000s of tips but to make the book as strong as possible I shared my top 100.

That will improve your brand or business instantly.
Contact me at
www.jalenhamilton.com

www.ingramcontent.com/pod-product-compliance
Lightning Source LLC
Chambersburg PA
CBHW030740180526
45157CB00008BA/3254